Catcher Charlie O'Brien

THE STORY OF THE TORONTO BLUE JAYS

Center fielder George Springer

THE STORY OF THE
TORONTO BLUE JAYS

JOE TISCHLER

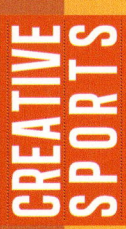

Shortstop Bo Bichette

CREATIVE EDUCATION / CREATIVE PAPERBACKS

Published by Creative Education and Creative Paperbacks
P.O. Box 227, Mankato, Minnesota 56002
Creative Education and Creative Paperbacks are imprints of
The Creative Company
www.thecreativecompany.us

Book Design by Wyeth Morgan
Art direction by Blue Design (www.bluedes.com)

Images by Alamy Stock Photo/JOHN ANGELILLO, 6 (bottom, right); Getty Images/Abelimages, 26–27, Alex Trautwig, 25, Bernstein Associates, 19, CARLO ALLEGRI, 1, Charles Ruppmann/New York Daily News Archive, 12, Doug Griffin, 15, George Tiedemann, 18, JEFF HAYNES, 7 (top, left), Jim McIsaac, 6 (bottom, left), Julian Avram/Icon Sportswire, 3, Larry W. Smith, 20, Mark Blinch, 29, Mary DeCicco, 2, MLB Photos, 16, Nick Cammett/Diamond Images, cover, 30, Rich Pilling, 7 (bottom, left), Rick Eglinton, 10, Rick Stewart, cover, 4–5, 6 (top, left), 10, 22–23, 32, Rob Skeoch, 7 (bottom, right), Rob Tringali, 31, Ron Vesely, 7 (top, right), Stephen Dunn, 6 (top, right), 9; Shutterstock/Lucky-photographer, 11

Every effort has been made to contact copyright holders for material reproduced in this book. Any omissions will be rectified in subsequent printings if notice is given to the publisher.

Copyright © 2026 Creative Education, Creative Paperbacks International copyright reserved in all countries. No part of this book may be reproduced in any form without written permission from the publisher.

Library of Congress Cataloging-in-Publication Data
Names: Tischler, Joe author
Title: The story of the Toronto Blue Jays / Joe Tischler.
Description: Mankato, Minnesota : Creative Education and Creative Paperbacks, [2026] | Series: Creative sports: Major League Baseball | Includes index. | Audience: Ages 8-12 | Audience: Grades 4-6 | Summary: "Discover the Toronto Blue Jays' thrilling journey from early struggles to World Series victories and recent playoff appearances, featuring star players, iconic moments, and the Major League Baseball team's passionate fanbase. Written for middle-grade readers. Includes table of contents, sidebars, and index"– Provided by publisher.
Identifiers: LCCN 2025019612 (print) | LCCN 2025019613 (ebook) | ISBN 9798895811122 library binding | ISBN 9798896800651 paperback | ISBN 9798895812389 ebook
Subjects: LCSH: Toronto Blue Jays (Baseball team)–Juvenile literature | Baseball–Ontario–Juvenile literature
Classification: LCC GV875.T67 T57 2026 (print) | LCC GV875.T67 (ebook) | DDC 796.357/6409713541–dc23/eng/20250708
LC record available at https://lccn.loc.gov/2025019612
LC ebook record available at https://lccn.loc.gov/2025019613

Printed in the United States

Second baseman Roberto Alomar

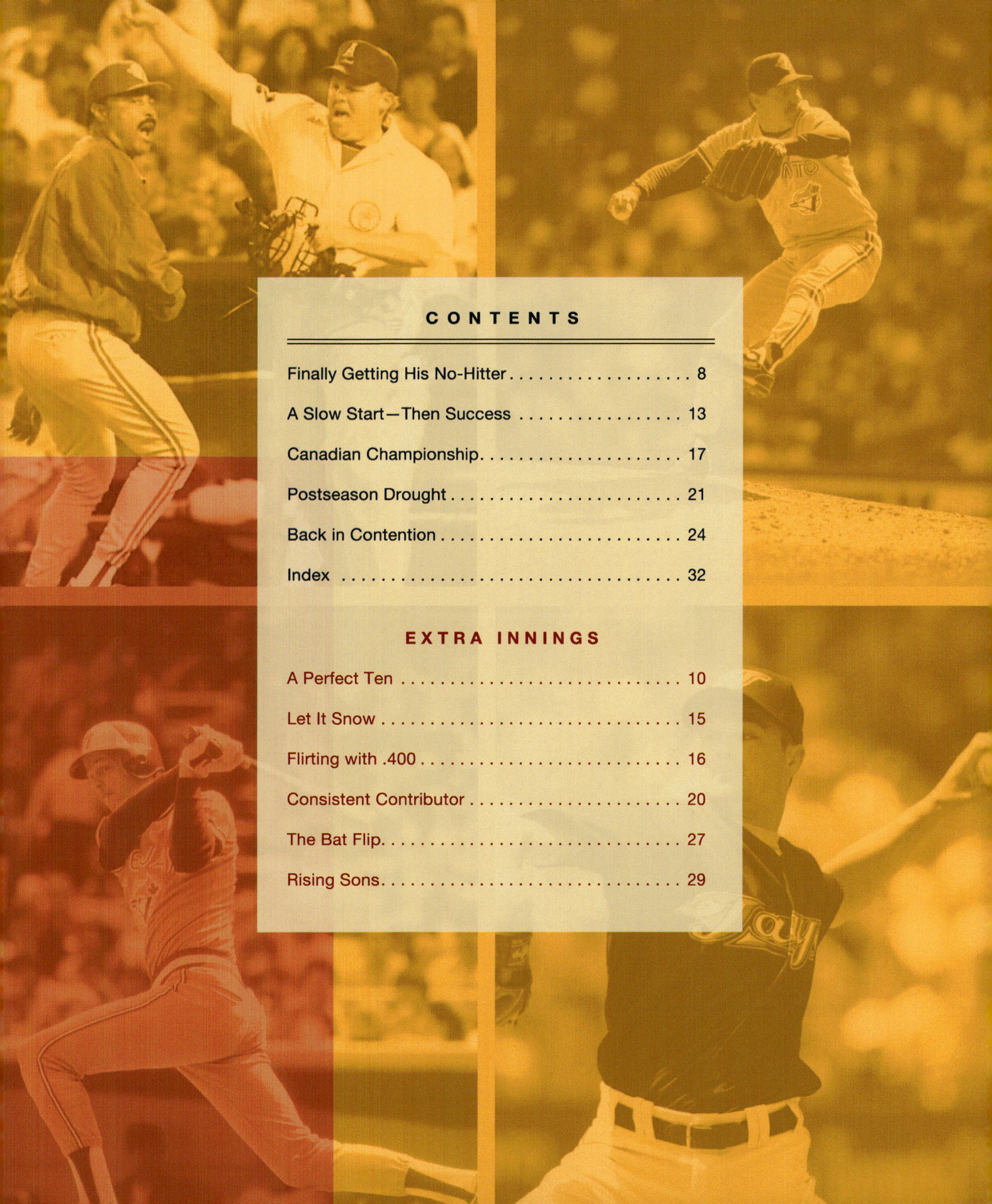

CONTENTS

Finally Getting His No-Hitter 8

A Slow Start—Then Success 13

Canadian Championship 17

Postseason Drought 21

Back in Contention 24

Index 32

EXTRA INNINGS

A Perfect Ten 10

Let It Snow 15

Flirting with .400 16

Consistent Contributor 20

The Bat Flip 27

Rising Sons 29

FINALLY GETTING HIS NO-HITTER

Dave Stieb did not have much pitching experience before making his major-league debut with the Toronto Blue Jays in 1979. Stieb primarily played outfield in college at Southern Illinois University. He was used sparingly as a pitcher, only tossing 17 innings. The Blue Jays told him the quickest way to get to the big leagues would be as a pitcher. He worked his way quickly through the Blue Jays farm system. Toronto selected him in the 1978 Major League Baseball (MLB) Draft. It took Stieb just one year to make it to the big leagues.

Stieb made his first All-Star team in 1980. He made four more All-Star teams in the next five years. He showed his durability during starts. He threw at least 11 complete games every year from 1980 to 1984. Stieb led the league with 19 complete games in 1982.

Stieb would come to be best known for flirting with no-hitters, only to lose them in the ninth inning. His first instance of a near "no-no" came in an August 1985 game at the Chicago White Sox. He threw eight no-hit innings. The first two batters for Chicago in the ninth inning hit home runs. Stieb was replaced. Toronto won 6–3.

Pitcher Dave Stieb

TORONTO BLUE JAYS

EXTRA INNINGS

**BALTIMORE ORIOLES AT TORONTO BLUE JAYS
SEPTEMBER 14, 1987**

A PERFECT TEN

The balls were flying out of Toronto's Exhibition Stadium on this September night. Catcher Ernie Whitt (right) led off the second inning with a home run. Third baseman Rance Mulliniks and center fielder Lloyd Moseby each added home runs in the inning. Left fielder George Bell and Mulliniks hit home runs in the third. Whitt added another blast in the fifth. Bell added his second long ball in the sixth. Whitt connected with his third deep shot in the seventh. Outfielder Rob Ducey hit one as well in the seventh. First baseman Fred McGriff added his own in the eighth. Toronto won the game 18–3 with the help of 10 home runs. That is an MLB record for team home runs in a game. "We might not ever again see a game like that," said manager Cito Gaston.

Toronto Skyline

In 1988, Stieb flirted with two no-hitters at the end of the season. On September 24, Stieb retired the first two Cleveland Indians' batters in the bottom of the ninth. He was just one out, and one strike away from a no-hitter. Julio Franco hit a ground ball toward second baseman Manny Lee. The ball hit a divot and bounced over his head. Stieb retired the next batter to preserve Toronto's 1–0 win. Six days later, Stieb again was mowing down opponent batters. He carried another no-hitter into the ninth inning against the Baltimore Orioles. Again, Stieb retired the first two batters. And, again, he was one strike away from recording his first no-hitter. But Baltimore's Jim Traber hit a solid single to right field to break up the no-hit bid. Stieb retired the next batter. Toronto won 4–0.

The following season, Stieb had a masterful performance in an August game against the New York Yankees. He had a perfect game through eight innings. He struck out the first two Yankees batters in the ninth inning. Those were Stieb's 10th and 11th strikeouts of the game. Roberto Kelly was New York's last hope for a base runner. He laced a 2–0 pitch down the left field line for a double. For the fourth time, Stieb's chance for a no-hitter was broken up in the ninth inning. Toronto won 2–1.

In September 1990, Stieb was in a familiar position. In a game at Cleveland, Stieb did not allow any hits through eight innings. Again, he retired the first two batters he faced. He was one out away from recording his elusive no-hitter. Jerry Browne was Cleveland's batter. He launched a fly ball to right. Junior Felix securely caught the ball. Stieb finally got his no-hitter! The Blue Jays won 3–0. "I've come to realize that there's just so much luck involved in a no-hitter," said Stieb. "That's what today was— all luck." As of 2024, it remains Toronto's only no-hitter in franchise history.

A SLOW START—THEN SUCCESS

In 1976, MLB voted to expand the American League (AL). Seattle and Toronto each received a franchise. In Canada, a naming contest drew 30,000 entries. Team official R. Howard Webster explained the final choice: "The blue jay is strong aggressive, and inquisitive. It dares to take on all comers, yet it is down-to-earth, gutsy, and good-looking."

The Blue Jays began playing in 1977. They defeated the Chicago White Sox in their opening game in front of the home Canadian fans. The team won five of its first seven games. After that, it won few games. Toronto lost 107 games its first season. The team sat in the AL East Division cellar for its first five seasons. Still, there were highlights. On September 10, 1977, third baseman Roy Howell drove in nine runs with five hits. The Blue Jays defeated the New York Yankees with a whopping 19 runs that day. Two years later, shortstop Alfredo Griffin collected 179 hits, 10 triples, and 81 runs. He earned AL co-Rookie of the Year honors.

Shortstop Alfredo Griffin

Toronto had some building blocks in place. The team steadily improved. Fiery pitcher Dave Stieb's brushback pitches whistled past batters. In the 1980s, second baseman Damaso Garcia teamed up with Griffin to turn frequent double plays. The bats of right fielder Jesse Barfield and first baseman Willie Upshaw began to heat up. Lloyd Moseby sped down the base paths.

The Blue Jays ended the 1983 season with their first winning record. The 89–73 mark was good enough for fourth place in the AL East. Toronto jumped to second place in 1984. It seemed that the Jays were ready to soar. The following season, they flew to 99 wins. Toronto won its first division title. It met the Kansas City Royals in the AL Championship Series (ALCS). The Blue Jays won three of the first four games. Then they fell apart. Kansas City won the final three games and the series.

Toronto took a step backward in its 10th season. Its pitchers struggled. But offensively, the team delivered. Shortstop Tony Fernandez smacked a club-record 213 hits. He posted a .319 batting average. Barfield led the major leagues with 40 home runs. Left fielder George Bell slugged 31 more. Still, the Jays' 86–76 record left them out of the playoffs.

FIRST BASEMAN DOUG AULT GIVES A KISS TO FAN DURING THE GAME DELAY

EXTRA INNINGS

LET IT SNOW

Exhibition Stadium served as the Blue Jays first home stadium. It also hosted Canadian Football League games. It was less than ideal for baseball. The stadium stood next to Lake Ontario. Icy winds and snow flurries often plagued fans early in the season. Yet, almost 45,000 fans turned out in these conditions for the team's first game. Snow covered the field before and during the game. The Blue Jays had to borrow the Zamboni from Maple Leaf Gardens (home of the National Hockey League's Maple Leafs) to clear off the field. To this date, it is the only MLB game to be played on a snow-covered field. Blue Jays first baseman Doug Ault hit two home runs in front of the home crowd. The Blue Jays defeated Chicago, 9–5.

JOHN OLERUD
FIRST BASEMAN
BLUE JAYS SEASONS: 1989–96
HEIGHT: 6-FOOT-5
WEIGHT: 205 POUNDS
KEY STATS: 2X ALL-STAR, 2X WORLD SERIES CHAMPION, 3X GOLD GLOVE, BATTING TITLE

FLIRTING WITH .400

John Olerud's baseball career nearly ended while he was in college. He suffered a severe brain condition. Olerud underwent surgery early in 1989. He continued playing. He always wore a batting helmet in the field for protection. The Blue Jays drafted him later that year. He went straight to the team without playing in the minor leagues. By 1993, Olerud had adjusted to the big leagues. "I'm more aggressive early in the count," he said of his hitting. He carried a .402 average into August. Olerud cooled off late in the season. Still, he finished with a .363 average. He became the first Toronto player to win the AL batting title.

CANADIAN CHAMPIONSHIP

In 1987, Toronto posted a 96–66 mark. It was the second-best MLB record that year. Bell won the AL Most Valuable Player (MVP) award. He hammered 47 home runs and batted in 134 runs (RBI). Unfortunately, the team played in the same division as the 98–64 Detroit Tigers. The Blue Jays missed out on the playoffs. They started slowly in 1988. They fell far behind in the division race by mid-July. After a late-season surge, they ended in third place.

The Blue Jays started the 1989 season 12–24. Then the team's hitting coach, Cito Gaston, was promoted to manager. He was a personable leader. "One thing I did learn as a player," Gaston said, "is that a manager should try to be honest with the team. If he is going to make a change, he should talk to the players involved. I respect the players, and I hope they respect me."

Gaston's style seemed to work. The Jays topped the AL East. But they lost to the Oakland Athletics in the ALCS. In 1990, nearly 3.9 million fans attended home games at SkyDome. The retractable roof stadium opened in June the previous season. That broke the MLB single-season attendance record. Toronto finished second place in the AL East. The following season, Toronto became the first baseball franchise to draw more than four million fans. The team traded for Joe Carter that year. It also signed versatile second baseman Roberto Alomar. The additions helped the Blue Jays win the AL East. But they lost to the Minnesota Twins in the ALCS.

In 1992, the Blue Jays assembled an impressive collection of talent. Newcomers included pitchers Jack Morris and David Cone and 12-time All-Star right fielder Dave Winfield. Steady catcher Pat Borders continued to man

1992 World Series

home plate. First baseman John Olerud became a hot hitter. These players worked together to win another division title.

The Blue Jays met Oakland in the ALCS. The Athletics won Game 1 at SkyDome. But Toronto bounced back to win the next three games. Oakland took Game 5. Back in Toronto for Game 6, the Blue Jays won, 9–2, to win the series. That clinched their first World Series appearance. It also marked the first time a Canadian team reached the World Series.

Toronto faced the Atlanta Braves in the World Series. Like the ALCS, the Jays dropped Game 1 but came back to win the next three games. The Braves won Game 5. Game 6 was a nail-biter. In the 11th inning, Winfield delivered a 2-RBI double to give Toronto the lead. Atlanta scored one in the bottom of the inning. With the tying run on third base, closer Mike Timlin got the final out on a bunt groundout. The Blue Jays were world champions! "I've dreamed about this more times than I've gotten out of bed," Timlin said.

Pitcher Dave Stieb

TORONTO BLUE JAYS

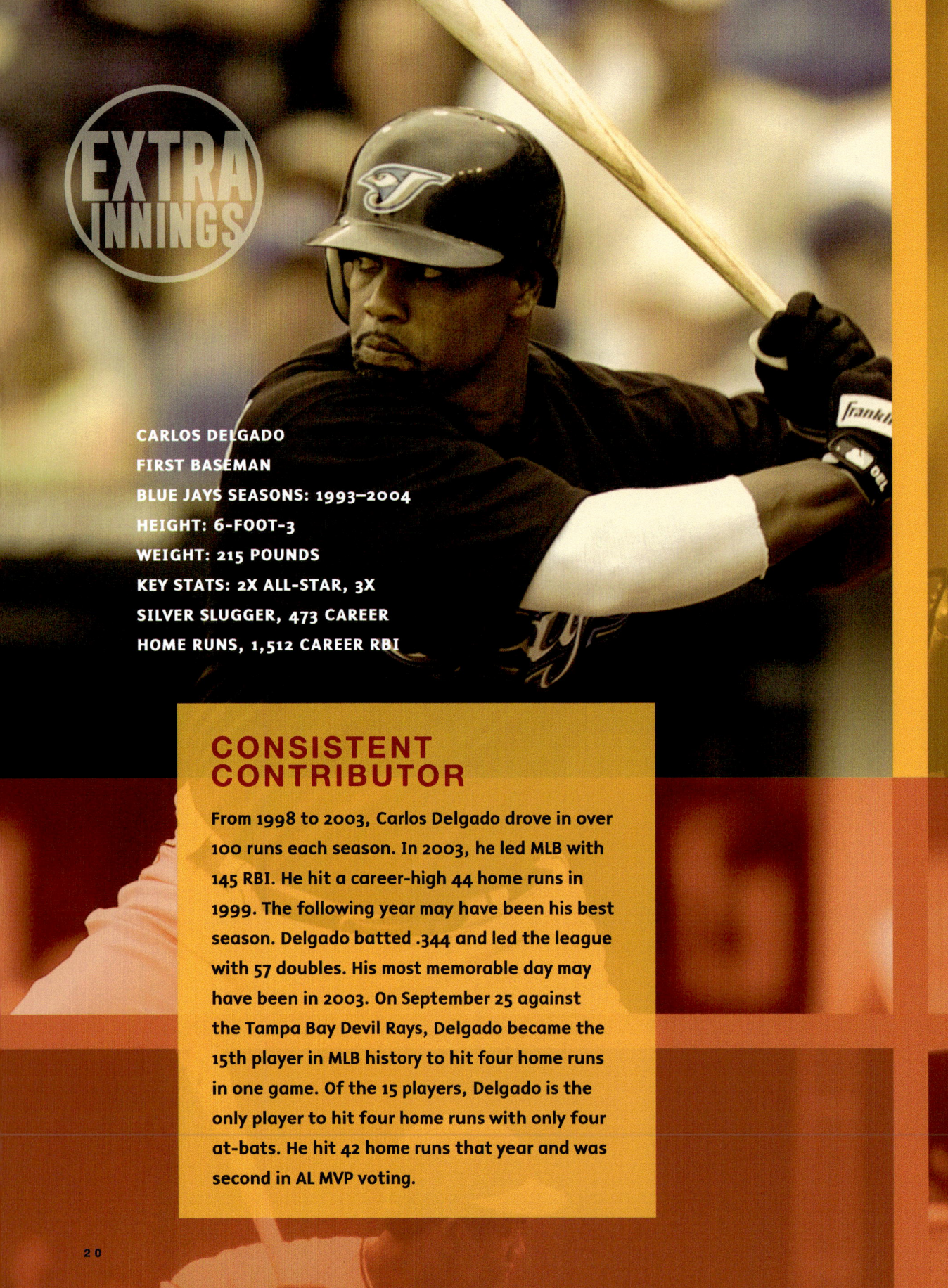

EXTRA INNINGS

CARLOS DELGADO
FIRST BASEMAN
BLUE JAYS SEASONS: 1993–2004
HEIGHT: 6-FOOT-3
WEIGHT: 215 POUNDS
KEY STATS: 2X ALL-STAR, 3X SILVER SLUGGER, 473 CAREER HOME RUNS, 1,512 CAREER RBI

CONSISTENT CONTRIBUTOR

From 1998 to 2003, Carlos Delgado drove in over 100 runs each season. In 2003, he led MLB with 145 RBI. He hit a career-high 44 home runs in 1999. The following year may have been his best season. Delgado batted .344 and led the league with 57 doubles. His most memorable day may have been in 2003. On September 25 against the Tampa Bay Devil Rays, Delgado became the 15th player in MLB history to hit four home runs in one game. Of the 15 players, Delgado is the only player to hit four home runs with only four at-bats. He hit 42 home runs that year and was second in AL MVP voting.

POSTSEASON DROUGHT

The high-flying Jays added several new players in 1993. They included designated hitter Paul Molitor and hard-throwing hurler Dave Stewart. Toronto soared to a 95–67 record. It captured the AL East for the third year in a row. The Blue Jays defeated the White Sox in the ALCS. The win sent Toronto to the World Series for the second year in a row.

The Blue Jays faced the Philadelphia Phillies in the World Series. Molitor had an outstanding series. He had 12 hits in 24 at-bats (.500 average). Half of his hits went for extra bases. He was named series MVP. Toronto led the series 3-2. It trailed Game 6 in Toronto, 6–5, going to the bottom of the ninth inning. The Phillies brought in closer Mitch Williams to pitch. Blue Jays center fielder Rickey Henderson walked to lead off the inning. Two batters later, Molitor singled to center to move Henderson to second. Carter came up to bat. He launched a line drive down the left field line that cleared the wall for a home run. The Blue Jays won 8–6. They were world champions again! Carter's home run marked the second time a World Series ended with a home run.

The Blue Jays hoped for a three-peat in 1994. But the team had a losing record of 55–60. A players' strike ended the season in August. In 1995, the team limped to a 56–88 record. It finished in the AL East cellar for the first time since 1981.

The team had stellar pitching the rest of the decade. But it did not create any playoff appearances. Pat Hentgen was a 20-game winner in 1996. He led MLB with 10 complete games and three shutouts. He won the AL Cy Young Award as the league's best pitcher. Toronto signed Roger Clemens before the

Right fielder Jesse Barfield

1997 season. He earned his fourth and fifth AL Cy Young Awards in his two Toronto seasons. Clemens earned the pitching Triple Crown both seasons, leading the league in wins, strikeouts, and earned run average (ERA).

Another dominant pitcher emerged in 2002. Roy Halladay served up a baffling assortment of fastballs and curveballs. He won 19 games that year. He improved to 22 wins in 2003. That earned him the AL Cy Young Award.

The team produced some hitting stars. Powerful first baseman Carlos Delgado had a stellar 2000 season with a .344 batting average, 41 home runs, and 137 RBI. Third baseman Eric Hinske was named AL Rookie of the Year in 2003. Frank Thomas notched his 500th career home run with the team in 2007.

BACK IN CONTENTION

The Blue Jays continued with their postseason drought into the 2010s. Before the 2013 season, a combination of free-agent signings and trades gave the Jays established stars. They included pitchers Josh Johnson and Mark Buehrle, infielder Maicer Izturis, and outfielder Melky Cabrera. Unfortunately, the team finished in last place in the AL East. The team rebounded to 83–79 the following year. After the season, the team acquired All-Star third baseman Josh Donaldson.

In 2015, the Blue Jays acquired two more All-Stars midseason. The newcomers were shortstop Troy Tulowitzki and pitcher David Price. Donaldson drove in a league-high 123 runs. He was named AL MVP. The players helped

Shortstop Troy Tulowitzki (right)

JOSE BAUTISTA
RIGHT FIELDER/THIRD BASEMAN
BLUE JAYS SEASONS: 2008–17
HEIGHT: 6-FOOT-0
WEIGHT: 205 POUNDS
KEY STATS: 6X ALL-STAR, 3X SILVER SLUGGER, 2X
HOME RUN LEADER, 344 CAREER HOME RUNS

THE BAT FLIP

Jose Bautista was not considered a home-run hitter early in his career. He had only 59 home runs through his first six seasons. Bautista erupted in 2010. He belted 54 home runs. The following year he hit 43. Bautista led MLB in home runs both seasons. In 2015, Bautista hit 40 home runs. His most memorable long shot came in Game 5 of the ALDS against Texas. In a tie game in the seventh inning, Bautista belted a three-run home run that hit off the facing of the second deck at Rogers Centre. As he hit the ball, Bautista stood at home plate then flipped the bat toward the dugout. This act made Texas mad. When the teams played the following season, Bautista was intentionally hit by a pitch as a form of retaliation.

propel Toronto to 93–69. It topped the AL East. It marked Toronto's first playoff appearance since 1993.

The Jays faced the Texas Rangers in the AL Division Series (ALDS). Toronto lost the first two games at home. It won Games 3 and 4 in Texas to send the series back to Toronto for a deciding fifth game. A Jose Bautista mammoth three-run home run in the seventh inning helped give Toronto a 6–3 win. The Blue Jays met Kansas City in the ALCS. The Royals grabbed the pennant with a 4–2 series win.

The following season, Toronto earned a spot in the Wild Card game. It faced the Baltimore Orioles. Designated hitter Edwin Encarnacion smashed a three-run home run in the bottom of the 11th inning. It gave Toronto the win. In the ALDS, the Blue Jays faced Texas again. They swept the Rangers in three games. Next, they faced the Cleveland Indians in the ALCS. The teams combined for just 20 runs in the 5-game series. Cleveland won, 4 games to 1.

The Jays fell short of the playoffs the next three seasons. In 2019, the team notched 247 home runs. It was the second-highest total in franchise history. Thirteen players hit 10 or more. Toronto's pitchers surrendered 228 home runs. It was the most in team history. The result was a 67–95 record.

Young stars helped Toronto win more in the 2020s. Infielders Vladimir Guerrero Jr. and Bo Bichette added punch at the plate. Robbie Ray was a quality starting pitcher. The 2020 season was shortened to 60 games because of the COVID-19 pandemic. The number of teams to make the playoffs went from five in each league to eight. This helped Toronto as their 32–28 record gave them the final spot in the AL playoffs. It was a quick postseason for Toronto, though, as they were swept by the Tampa Bay Rays in the best-of-three AL Wild Card (ALWC) series.

Guerrero Jr. had a monster 2021 season. He batted .311 with a league-leading 48 home runs. He was runner-up in AL MVP voting. Second baseman Marcus Semien belted 45 home runs of his own. He was third in AL MVP voting.

FIRST BASEMAN VLADIMIR GUERRERO JR.

RISING SONS

Toronto finished 2019 with a disappointing record. But the team had three rays of hope. All were sons of former baseball stars. Vladimir Guerrero Jr. led AL rookies with 126 hits. His dad, Vladimir Sr., won an MVP award and is in the Hall of Fame. Bo Bichette set an MLB record with a double in nine straight games. His dad, Dante, was a four-time All-Star. Cavan Biggio became part of just the second father-son combination to hit for the cycle. His dad, Craig, is in the Hall of Fame. Guerrero Jr. and Bichette are two of the best young hitters in the game and have reached multiple All-Star games. Biggio was fifth in AL Rookie of the Year in 2019. He was traded from the team in 2024.

Pitcher Kevin Gausman

Guerrero Jr., Siemen, Bichette, and outfielder Teoscar Hernandez all drove in over 100 runs. On the mound, Ray was named the AL Cy Young Award winner. He led the league in both ERA (2.84) and strikeouts (248). The Blue Jays won 91 games. But they finished just one game out of a wild card berth.

Alek Manoah burst onto the scene in 2022. The 24-year-old starting pitcher won 16 games. The All-Star was third in AL Cy Young voting. Toronto won 92 games and qualified for the playoffs as a wild card. But they fell to the Seattle Mariners in the ALWC series. Toronto returned to the playoffs again in 2023. But it was another quick playoff exit as they were swept by Minnesota in the ALWC series. The Blue Jays fell back in the standings in 2024. They were 74–88 and finished last in the AL East.

In a dramatic turnaround, the Blue Jays finished the 2025 season with a 94–68 record, won the AL East, and advanced through the playoffs to reach the 2025 World Series. It was their first appearance since 1993. They lost to the Los Angeles Dodgers in an exciting seven-game series. Game 7 went into extra innings.

Since 1977, Toronto has been a great place for baseball. With stellar leadership and sound personnel decisions, the team can never be counted out. After celebrating back-to-back World Series titles in the 1990s, Toronto fans eagerly await the Blue Jays' next flight to championship territory.

Second baseman Andres Gimenez

INDEX

AL Championship Series (ALCS), 14, 17, 18, 21, 28
AL Division Series (ALDS), 27, 28
AL Wild Card Series (ALWC), 28, 31
Alomar, Roberto, 4, 17
Ault, Doug, 15
Barfield, Jesse, 14, 23
Bautista, Jose, 27, 28
Bell, George, 10, 14, 17
Bichette, Bo, 3, 28, 29, 31
Biggio, Cavan, 29
Borders, Pat, 17
Buehrle, Mark, 24
Cabrera, Melky, 24
Carter, Joe, 17, 21
Clemens, Roger, 21, 24
Cone, David, 17
COVID-19, 28
Cy Young Award, 21, 24, 31
Delgado, Carlos, 20, 24
Donaldson, Josh, 24
Ducey, Rob, 10
Encarnacion, Edwin, 28
Exhibition Stadium, 10, 15
Felix, Junior, 13
Fernandez, Tony, 14
Garcia, Damaso, 14
Gaston, Cito, 10, 17
Griffin, Alfredo, 13, 14
Guerrero, Vladimir, Jr., 28, 29, 31
Halladay, Roy, 24
Henderson, Rickey, 21
Hentgen, Pat, 21
Hernandez, Teoscar, 31
Hinske, Eric, 24
Howell, Roy, 13
Izturis, Maicer, 24
Johnson, Josh, 24
Lee, Manny, 11
Manoah, Alek, 31
McGriff, Fred, 10
MLB Draft, 8
Molitor, Paul, 21
Morris, Jack, 17
Moseby, Lloyd, 10, 14
Most Valuable Player (MVP), 17, 20, 21, 24, 28, 29
Mulliniks, Rance, 10
no-hitter, 8, 11, 13
Olerud, John, 16, 18
Price, David, 24
Ray, Robbie, 28, 31
Rogers Centre (SkyDome), 17, 18, 27
Rookie of the Year, 13, 24, 29
Semien, Marcus, 28
Stewart, Dave, 21
Stieb, Dave, 8, 9, 11, 13, 14, 19
team name, 13
Thomas, Frank, 24
Timlin, Mike, 18
Triple Crown, 24
Tulowitzki, Troy, 24
Upshaw, Willie, 14
Webster, R. Howard, 13
Whitt, Ernie, 10
Winfield, Dave, 17, 18
World Series, 16, 18, 21, 31
World Series champions, 16, 18, 21